SCHOLASTIC Phonics

AF095831

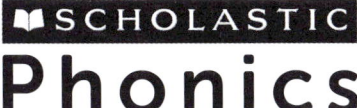

Go Wild!

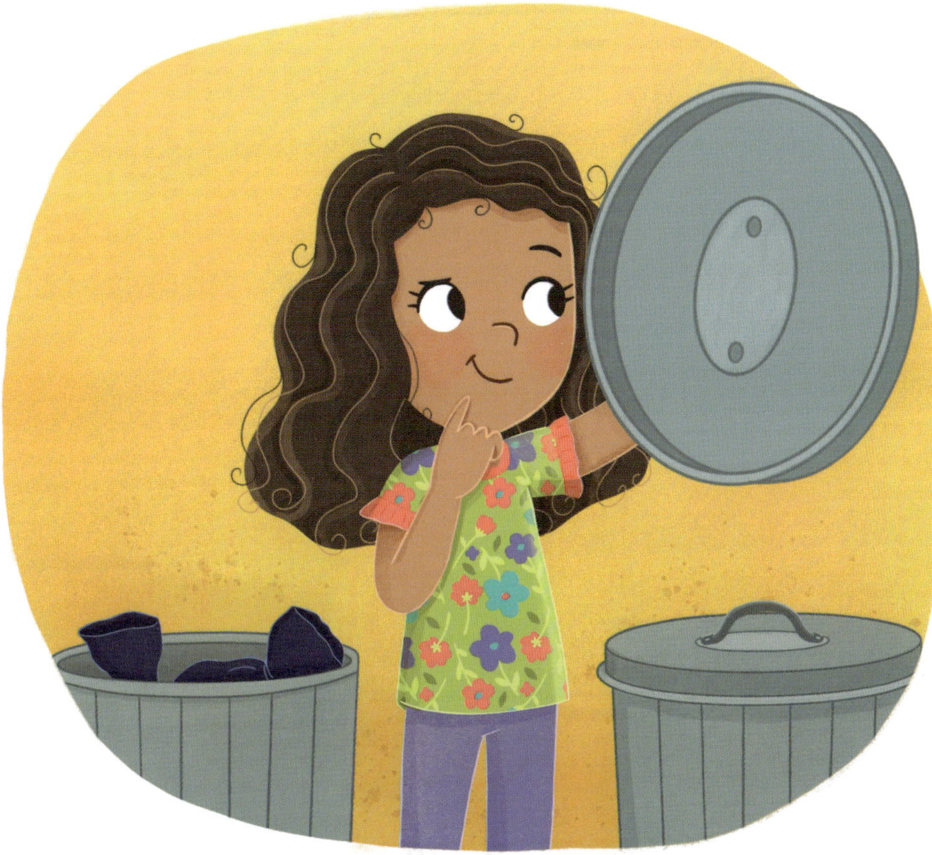

Published in the UK by Scholastic Education, 2022
Scholastic Distribution Centre, Bosworth Avenue, Tournament Fields, Warwick, CV34 6UQ
Scholastic Ireland, 89E Lagan Road, Dublin Industrial Estate, Glasnevin, Dublin, D11 HP5F

SCHOLASTIC and associated logos are trademarks and/or registered trademarks of Scholastic Inc.
www.scholastic.co.uk
© 2022 Scholastic
1 2 3 4 5 6 7 8 9   2 3 4 5 6 7 8 9 0 1

Printed by Ashford Colour Press
The book is made of materials from well-managed, FSC®-certified forests and other controlled sources.

A CIP catalogue record for this book is available from the British Library.

ISBN 978-0702-30916-8

All rights reserved. This book is sold subject to the condition that it shall not, by way of trade or otherwise, be lent, hired out or otherwise circulated in any form of binding or cover other than that in which it is published. No part of this publication may be reproduced, stored in a retrieval system, or transmitted in any form or by any other means (electronic, mechanical, photocopying, recording or otherwise) without prior written permission of Scholastic Limited.

Every effort has been made to trace copyright holders for the works reproduced in this publication, and the publishers apologise for any inadvertent omissions.

Author
Ann Hill
Editorial team
Rachel Morgan, Vicki Yates, Fiona Undrill, Jennie Clifford
Design team
Dipa Mistry, Justin Hoffmann, Andrea Lewis, We Are Grace
Illustrations
Brenda Figueroa/Plum Pudding Illustration

Help your child to read!

This book practises these letters and letter sounds.
Point and say the sounds with your child:

- o (as in 'go')
- i (as in 'wild')
- a (as in 'baking')
- e (as in 'she')
- a-e (as in 'make')
- i-e (as in 'five')
- o-e (as in 'note')
- u-e (as in 'tune')
- ew (as in 'blew')
- ie (as in 'cookies')
- aw (as in 'sawed')

Your child may need help to read these common tricky words:

- by
- said
- something
- to
- into
- want
- the
- could
- they
- what
- are
- you
- was

Before reading
- Look at the cover picture and read the title together. Read the back cover blurb to your child.
- Ask your child: *Have you been to an event like this?*

During reading
- If your child gets stuck on a word, remind them to sound it out and then blend the sounds to read the word: w-i-l-d, wild.
- If they are still stuck, show them how to read the word.
- Enjoy looking at the pictures together. Pause to talk about the story.

After reading
- Ask your child: *What did Ellie make to go wild? Do you think it was a good idea?*
- Ask your child if they have any ideas about how they could make a musical instrument. (Perhaps you could make one together.)

Ellie is thrilled by this year's festival theme.

"I'm baking a dragon cake," said Grandad.

Dad blew into his trombone.
Ellie made up her mind.
"I want to make wild music for the festival," she said.

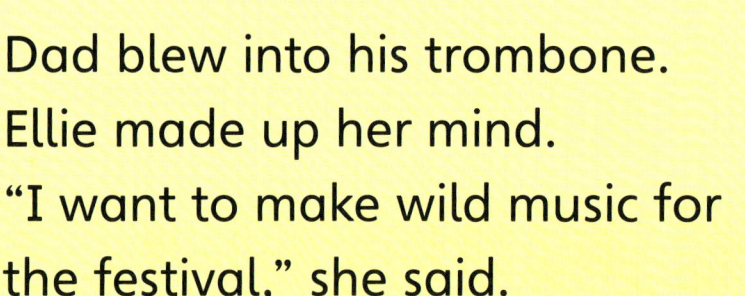

"Find something in the music box," said Mum.

Ellie blew into a flute but could not make a note.

She tried to make a tune on the banjo. The strings broke.

I wish I had a drum set.

Ellie threw away the rubbish.

Gazing at the bin lids,
Ellie came up with a plan.

She unscrewed lids off old jars.

Grandad gave her an old case.

Ellie spoke to Lewis, the repair man. He sawed five pipes.

Ellie and her dad had a wild plan. They took tools, a saw, lids and bits behind the shed.

"What *are* you making?" shrieked Mum.
"A wild thing!" yelled Ellie.

Ellie's amazing wild drum kit was finished just in time for the festival.

What a wild time!
Grandad gave out dragon cake and flame-red cookies.
Tigers with soft paws chased lions with felt claws.

Dad's trombone and Ellie's drum made the wildest music ever!

Retell the story